D0471366

Dedicated to John Darby, champion of the hoiho,
and to all who are helping to save endangered species
and their habitats.

What is man without the beasts? If all the beasts
were gone, man would die from a great loneliness of
spirit. For whatever happens to the beasts soon
happens to man. All things are connected.
—CHIEF SEATTLE

THE HOIHO

New Zealand's Yellow-Eyed Penguin

by ADELE VERNON

photographs by DEAN SCHNEIDER

WWF

G. P. Putnam's Sons, New York

Author's Note

This book is based on personal observations of the hoiho that live in forest remnants along the Southeast coast of New Zealand. Behavior may differ depending on habitat conditions. New research is constantly updating our knowledge about this unusual penguin.

Maori names for animals, plants and places have been italicized. In accordance with the Maori language, there is no plural form of nouns.

Acknowledgments

Enormous thanks to zoologist John Darby, who has been conducting research on the hoiho and its habitat since 1980, and has been instrumental in the recovery program. He has generously shared his information and has made valuable comments on the text. I also wish to acknowledge the ground-breaking studies on the hoiho by the late Dr. Lance E. Richdale, as well as Dr. Philip Seddon's work and the Department of Conservation's management plan. Many thanks to Jane Thomson and Dr. John Hall-Jones for reading the text. We are indebted to coastal farmers who allowed us to spend hours on their land observing the hoiho from bird hides. We appreciate Kodak's assistance with Kodacrome 64, and the grant from Mobil Oil for the purchase of some film. The support of family, in particular Erik and Martina, and friends has been greatly appreciated. We are especially grateful to our editors, Anne O'Connell, Caroline Press and Tom Beran, for their enthusiasm, guidance and patience. Special recognition to all those who are helping to save the hoiho. Finally a lasting acknowledgment of appreciation and respect for the remarkable hoiho.

Photo Credits

Thanks to Geoff Moon (kiwi photo) and Rod Morris (feral cat photo).

The authors of this book have kindly agreed to make a contribution to the World Wildlife Fund's efforts to protect the hoiho. ® WWF Registered Trade Mark Owner.

Library of Congress Cataloging-in-Publication Data: Vernon, Adele. The hoiho, New Zealand's yellow-eyed penguin / by Adele Vernon; photographs by Dean Schneider. p. cm. Summary: Discusses New Zealand's forest-dwelling penguin, rarest of the world's penguins and edging closer to extinction every year. 1. Yellow-eyed penguin—New Zealand—Juvenile literature. [1. Yellow-eyed penguin. 2. Penguins.] I. Schneider, Dean, ill. II. Title. QL696.S473V45 1991 598'.441—dc20 90-8097 CIP AC ISBN 0-399-21686-3
10 9 8 7 6 5 4 3 2 1 First Impression

Foreword

THE HOIHO, New Zealand's yellow-eyed penguin, has become a symbol of hope in the continuing efforts to save the many threatened bird species of New Zealand.

During millions of years of isolation from the rest of the world, these ancient islands, cloaked in lush rain forest and free of mammalian predators, were a paradise for a unique bird life. But a thousand years of human colonization has drastically altered this fragile natural environment. The relentless destruction of forests and the importation of predators and other animals has had a disastrous impact on native birds. Today only 23% of the land is covered in forest as compared to 80% a thousand years ago. More than half the country's original complement of bird species is either extinct or endangered.

Assisted by New Zealand's largest conservation group, the Royal Forest and Bird Protection Society, the rescue of some critically at-risk birds is well under way, and attention has now focused on other threatened species. One of these is a reclusive, forest-dwelling penguin, the hoiho.

Due to habitat loss, predation and starvation their population has plummeted to fewer than 5000. Warnings about the plight of the hoiho struck a sympathetic chord with environmentalists, writer Adele Vernon and photographer Dean Schneider, who have dedicated more than eight years to observing, photographing, describing and protecting this unique penguin who is their neighbor. Because of their work and that of many others, the name "hoiho" has become a household word in New Zealand. In turn the welfare and survival of these endearing birds has been taken up by communities, organizations and individuals throughout the country.

In a world facing unprecedented environmental crises the hoiho story stands out as a shining example of people working together to protect a fellow creature of the planet earth.

DR. GERRY McSWEENEY, *Director*
Royal Forest and Bird Protection Society of New Zealand

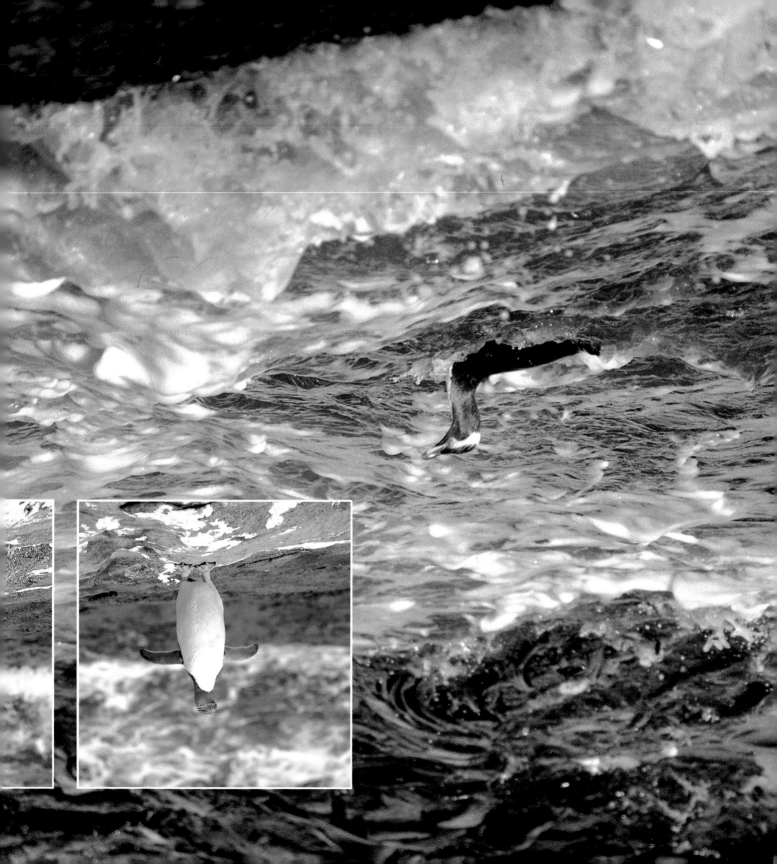

A lone penguin wings swiftly through the frothy kelp-strewn waves that lash the jagged coast. Grappling with nail-sharp claws, bill and flippers, she gets a foothold on the slippery rock, hops upright and scrambles ashore before the next surge of the sea can send her tumbling back. With keen yellow eyes she quickly surveys the landing area where the spring light of a blustery September afternoon is already fading. Nearby three juvenile penguins are splashing about in the pool of a freshwater stream. After a flipper-reaching stretch and a few tail-flicking shakes, the glistening wet bird briefly preens her brilliant white and slate-blue coat. Her yellow-banded head angles this way and that as she oils and grooms the short feathers with her large brownish-red bill.

Webbed feet flushed to a bright pink, the penguin soon sets off with a brisk waddling gait down the rocky shore. Just ahead two jet-black *torea-pango* are scurrying about patrolling their nesting territory. Shrill "kervee, kervee" warnings spill from these oyster catchers as the intruder approaches. But the penguin is in a hurry. She glances at the noisy pair, then slips into the stream. After a short swim inland, the penguin begins the long trek up a steep, windswept headland to her nest.

The short-legged traveler hops over boulders, struggles up slippery banks and clambers across fallen trees. The going is tough and she rests often along the trail to catch her breath and cool off. Creaking above her in the gusty sea winds are the skeletons of once great trees, reminders of the magnificent rain forest that once covered this wild, remote coast. Sheep flanked by "maaing" lambs are munching their way through the grass and scrub that now hug the hillsides. Piercing "kak, kak, kak" cries ricochet off the cliffs as *karoro,* the black-backed gulls, shriek and swoop above a colony of untidy nests where their chicks will weather the fierce South Pacific storms. Far below on the rocks, brown shapes begin to move about, stretching, scratching and yawning. They are *kekeno,* the fur seals, waking from an afternoon nap.

At last the penguin crests the hill and halts. Suddenly, flippers flung out and head thrown back, she gives a loud homecoming cry—"hoi-ho, hoi-ho." As she continues on her journey a curious lamb scampers up and sends her scuttling through a wire fence. Now over one-half mile from the

Trudging across denuded headlands that were once covered with lush forest, the nest-bound penguin is exposed to many dangers and difficulties before it is home.

sea, the penguin disappears into a surviving patch of forest. Tunneling through a tangle of vines, ferns and shrubs, she soon reaches the well-concealed nest at the base of an ancient hollow tree. Her mate, who has been waiting, rushes up to meet her. Yellow-banded heads shaking with excitement, the two penguins join in an exuberant duet of trills and calls, part of an elaborate greeting ceremony that is performed by mates throughout the year.

Down on the shore other yellow-eyed birds of the sea have been coming in for the night, singly or in twos and threes. Penguins with partners are soon heading nestward through the spring twilight. Before long the land-ing rock is left to the harried oyster catchers, a few juvenile penguins and those adults without mates. By nightfall the breeding ground echoes with the zestful cries of penguins welcoming each other in the leafy darkness of their hidden nests.

Ringing above the roar of the sea, the vibrant trilling calls of this forest-dwelling penguin were well known to the Maori, New Zealand's first human inhabitants. Long ago they named the secretive but loud singer *hoiho*, the noise shouter.

Today the hoiho is also known as the "yellow-eyed" penguin because it is the only member of the penguin family that has yellow eyes. Another distinctive feature of this tall, slender bird is the band of bright yellow feathers that encircles its head like a coronet. This head marking makes it easily recognizable, on land or at sea, to its fellows.

Scientists have given the handsome hoiho yet another name. Because it is so unlike all other penguins in both behavior and appearance, it has the honor of being the sole *species*, or member, of its own special *genus*, or group, *Megadyptes* (*Mega*—"big," *dyptes*—"diver"). The full scientific name is *Megadyptes antipodes*, "big diver from the southern lands." Stand-ing just over two feet tall and weighing from eleven to eighteen pounds, the hoiho is the fourth largest of the world's penguins and has been known to dive to depths of 300 feet.

This trilling, yellow-eyed big diver is found only in New Zealand. It makes its home along the southeast coast of the South Island and in the coastal forests of Stewart Island and a few offshore islets. In New Zealand's subantarctic region, the hoiho lives on the Auckland and Campbell Islands.

Because of its vibrant
musical calls, the Maori
named this tall handsome
yellow-eyed penguin hoiho,
the noise shouter.

NEW ZEALAND

Map showing where the Yellow-Eyed Penguin is found

Trekking off alone to a hidden nest in coastal forest or seaside scrub certainly seems to be strange behavior for a penguin—and it is. Most penguins are, in fact, very social birds that breed close together in teeming noisy colonies where there is little more than shuffling space between nests. Although some colonies are relatively small, others are immense, like those of the familiar Adelie penguin in the antarctic region. On the bleak landscapes where many penguins raise their young, they are buffeted by severe storms and assailed by aerial predators such as *skuas,* large gull-like birds. But life in a colony has communal advantages: besides warmth in huddling, there is safety in numbers. A great congregation of penguins squawking, flailing their hard flippers and stabbing with sharp bills has a better chance of warding off an attack than a lone bird.

The majority of penguins, however, do not live at their crowded colony sites all year long. After the breeding season and yearly molt, they head out to the open sea where they spend the rest of the year fishing in groups. When it is time to breed again, the penguins return to their home colonies where they stake out nesting territories.

How very different the private family life of the New Zealand hoiho is from this crowded existence. Instead of massing together in large open colonies, these penguins seek out sheltered nests completely isolated from those of their neighbors. Compared with the many thousands of nests packed into a single Adelie colony, the number of nests scattered over a yellow-eyed penguin breeding ground is small, ranging from forty to as few as two. And unlike many of its relatives that spend the nonbreeding season at sea far from their colonies, the adult hoiho is a *sedentary*, "stay-at-home," penguin that lives on its breeding ground throughout the year. After fishing during the day, these yellow-eyed birds scrabble onto rocky shores or ride the surf onto sandy beaches to spend the night at or near their year-round nest sites.

But why did the hoiho, long ago, become such a hermit? In order to survive on land, this penguin needed protection not only from aerial predators and raging storms, but also from the heat of the sun which was especially acute during the summer breeding season. Like other members of the penguin family, the hoiho has a dense, waterproof coat and thick

For a penguin, a bird superbly designed for life in the sea, the hoiho spends a surprising amount of time on land—even more than it does in the water!

fat deposits which keep it dry and warm while fishing in the frigid South Pacific sea. Ordinarily, this thermal gear would have made such a tall, large-bodied penguin overdressed for life on land in a temperate climate like New Zealand's. But the hoiho was lucky. For many thousands of years these islands provided them with moist, dense evergreen forests that bordered the food-rich sea and were completely free of mammalian predators. Here was an ideal *habitat*, a place to live, for a flightless ground-nesting bird in need of shade as well as safety and shelter.

Beneath the leafy canopy of towering trees, deep in the green mosaic of shrubs and ferns, the hoiho found an abundance of cool, hidden nest sites. No attacking seabirds penetrated the forest fortress; no enemies lurked among the shadows. In this spacious haven there was no need to group together for mutual protection. The hoiho was threatened only at sea by predators such as sharks and seals. Life on land for this shy, trusting penguin was peaceful, private and leisurely.

The lush forests, where the hoiho made its home, had their origins long, long ago on the southern supercontinent of Gondwanaland. When the continental plates that make up the earth's crust began to shift, this vast giant split up into smaller landmasses. About 100 million years ago the islands which would one day be called *Aotearoa*, "land of the long white cloud," by the Maori, and "New Zealand" by the Europeans, drifted away into the southern sea with a precious cargo.

For millions of years New Zealand was a sanctuary for an unusual variety of plants and animals. Neither rats nor cats roamed these islands where the only mammals were small short-tailed bats. No snakes slithered through the greenness. Species survived here which are found nowhere else, like *tuatara*, a living fossil, the sole example of an extinct order of small nocturnal reptiles that evolved before the dinosaurs.

In the primeval forests of *kauri*, *kahikatea*, *rimu* and beech, strange and wonderful birds flourished. Among them were ancient flightless species, such as the long-billed *kiwi*, a shaggy night-forager, and *kakapo*, a large, secretive parrot of the twilight, which still survive in small numbers today. From the mountain stronghold of *kea*, the world's only alpine parrot, to the coastal forest hideaways of the hoiho, the land and its inhabitants sustained each other.

The hoiho evolved its solitary life-style, so unique among penguins, in ancient coastal forests, where it lived in peace and safety for millions of years. Now only straggly patches of forest remain for nesting.

Then one day humans discovered this rich isolated land. About 1000 years ago the Maori came by canoe from Polynesia, bringing rats and dogs with them. They lived off the land by hunting, gathering and gardening. With fire and tools they gradually began clearing the great forests. With weapons they hunted the trusting birds. But with the arrival of the Europeans some 150 years ago the destruction of the forests, the damage to the land and the assault on native birds greatly increased. Grazing and browsing animals, deadly predators and *noxious,* or harmful, plants were brought to this new unspoiled country. The peaceful life of the hoiho and other native birds came to an end. Some, like the twelve-foot high *moa,* the tallest bird that ever lived, the orange-wattled *huia,* and *hakoke,* the laughing owl, are extinct.

The hoiho is now at risk, on offshore islands as well as on the mainland. In little more than a century, a unique forest, millions of years old, that stretched hundreds of miles along the South Island's southeast coast was cut and burned to clear the land for farming and development. Many penguins perished in the raging fires that destroyed their homes. Today less than a mile of woodsy habitat is left. In the grass and meager scrub where the penguins try to nest, they suffer from heat stress and are

The flightless kiwi, *the only bird in the world with nostrils at the tip of its long bill, probes the forest litter, "smelling out" worms and other food to dig up.*

menaced by predators. The grazing of animals, like sheep, cattle and goats, further destroys their habitat by preventing the regeneration of plants and trees. Cattle barge through the breeding grounds, trampling nests, breaking eggs and frightening the penguins.

The settlers brought other animals such as cats, dogs and rabbits with them to make the strange new country seem more like home. Today *feral* cats, domestic cats that have gone wild, stalk nearly all of the hoiho's breeding grounds, including those on Stewart, Auckland and Campbell Islands, and kill both chicks and adults. Penguins trudging homeward over pastureland instead of in the shadowy safety of the forest, are ready prey for dogs out on the run. With no natural predators in New Zealand, the rabbit population exploded and acres of farmland were ruined. *Mustilids,* such as ferrets and stoats, were introduced to curb the burrowing pests. But when these rapacious hunters follow the rabbits onto the cleared land of the breeding grounds, they discover a plentiful and easily caught source of food—the poorly protected hoiho chicks.

Even at sea the hoiho is under threat. Plastic debris, fishing nets and oil pollution all take their toll. And in recent years large numbers of adults, juveniles and chicks have died of starvation. One reason for food shortages may be overfishing of squid and a variety of fish by huge commercial fleets. Another factor is the unusually warm ocean temperatures caused by El Niño, an abnormal recurring climate pattern which affects the food chain. The result is a decrease in the number of small fish that the hoiho feed on.

This rarest of penguins is edging closer and closer to extinction. Census surveys show that the hoiho population is declining steadily, particularly on the mainland where there are fewer than 500 pairs remaining. Scientists estimate that there are only about 5000 yellow-eyed penguins left in the world.

Penguins make up one of the oldest and most specialized bird families. They have lived on the planet earth for a very long time, much longer than humans, horses or seals. They have survived the earth's turbulent natural disasters, from the ice ages to volcanic upheavals, and nearly four and a half centuries of slaughter for their flesh, oil and skins at the hands of humans. By studying the fossil bones of penguins, *paleontologists* have determined that these extraordinary creatures appeared more than sixty

Killer cats and other predators are year-round threats to the trusting defenseless hoiho.

million years ago in the Southern Hemisphere, probably in the New Zealand biotic region. Penguin experts now think that the hoiho may be the most ancient of the seventeen species living today.

Fossil remains of the earliest penguins reveal that these seafaring birds and their closest relatives, the tube-nosed petrels and albatrosses, evolved from a common flying ancestor. Then why don't penguins fly?

An old Maori legend tells of *toroa,* an albatross, and *tawaki,* a crested penguin, who argued constantly about which one was better at flying and fishing. Finally, *Tane-mahuta,* the god of the forests and birds, got so tired of their squabbling that he separated the two and gave each one a unique gift. "*Toroa,* I present you with the longest wings of any seabird so that you can sail the ocean winds far from land in search of your food," boomed *Tane.* "And you, *tawaki,* will be the only bird to have these narrow, flipper-like wings. Now you can 'fly' beneath the ocean waves to catch the fish you need."

Although this is only a legend, there is some truth in it. Scientists explain that it probably took many thousands of years for the penguin to evolve into the flightless, submarine fisher we know today. While petrels and albatrosses specialized in flying, plunge-diving and surface feeding, penguins gradually lost their ability to fly through the air and became expert at swimming, diving and feeding underwater. By occupying this ecological niche they lessened the competition with flying birds for food.

Adaptations, or changes, occurred in the penguin's body and wings which allowed these birds to dive deeper and deeper and swim faster and faster. As the body became more robust and the bones got heavier and denser, diving became easier. The legs shifted further back on the oval-shaped body which made it more streamlined. Instead of the large, long-quilled feathered wings of other seabirds, penguins developed narrow, flat, tapered limbs that are densely covered with short, oily, scale-like feathers and cannot fold. When the penguin swims on the surface, duck like with its head up, these "flippers" are used like paddles. But when propelling the penguin swiftly underwater, they are held out from the body and make the same movements made by the wings of flying birds. Of all the birds in the world, only the penguin has these unique flipper-wings.

According to some authorities it is because the penguin's rigid, blade-

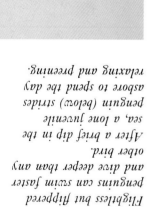

Flightless but flippered
penguins can swim faster
and dive deeper than any
other bird.
After a brief dip in the
sea, a lone juvenile
penguin (below) strides
ashore to spend the day
relaxing and preening.

like wing looks like a *spheniscus,* Latinized Greek for "little wedge," that the scientific name *Spheniscidae* was chosen for this largest family of flightless birds. Others suggest that the name refers to the wedge-shaped look of the penguin's body, from pointed bill to webbed feet.

Penguins—from the braying jackass to the hip-hopping rockhopper to the stately king—have a special fascination for people. At first glance they seem to be a strange composite of animals, like something from a myth. Penguins are birds with wings but they cannot fly. Instead they swim as gracefully as fish and make porpoising leaps through the waves like dolphins. But on land they walk upright, very much like humans. Because the short legs are placed far back on the body and the webbed feet are flat, the penguin clips along, head thrust forward and flippers held out for balance, with the curious rocking gait for which it is famous. Although often thought of as comical, clumsy little fellows, penguins can move with surprising speed and agility over rugged terrain. These remarkable birds live their difficult lives in two very different worlds: in the sea where they feed and on land where they raise their young.

The hoiho has one of the longest breeding seasons of any penguin. For about six and a half months mated pairs are devoted to family duties. The season begins in mid-August with the selection of mates, followed by the choosing and building of nests. It ends in late February to early March when the chicks are ready to go to sea.

Many yellow-eyed penguin couples stay together year after year. But sometimes pairs will change mates. One reason for this seems to be the failure to raise a family. Another reason may be incompatibility. Yellow-eyed penguins may look much the same, but as with all animals, individuals can have very different personalities. While most couples work well together and are devoted to each other, some birds just don't get along. But the main reason for a yellow-eyed penguin to seek a new mate is to replace a partner that dies.

Although partnerships are formed gradually and mates may be chosen anytime during the year, courting activities become more accelerated during the nonbreeding season, May to August, when the penguins have leisure time for socializing. The sedate yet intense drama of hoiho court-

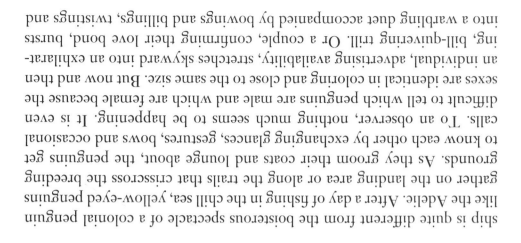

Juvenile penguins enthusiastically join in the courtship ritual by imitating adult trills and bows.

ship is quite different from the boisterous spectacle of a colonial penguin like the Adélie. After a day of fishing in the chill sea, yellow-eyed penguins gather on the landing area or along the trails that crisscross the breeding grounds. As they groom their coats and lounge about, the penguins get to know each other by exchanging glances, gestures, bows and occasional calls. To an observer, nothing much seems to be happening. It is even difficult to tell which penguins are male and which are female because the sexes are identical in coloring and close to the same size. But now and then an individual, advertising availability, stretches skyward into an exhilarating, bill-quivering trill. Or a couple, confirming their love bond, bursts into a warbling duet accompanied by bowings and billings, twistings and

The hoiho communicates with a wide range of flippered gestures and expressive calls.

turnings. These vocal displays, which have a musical quality quite unlike the jarring clamor of most other penguins, are part of a large repertoire of hoiho calls and postures.

A silent but very expressive bow, used casually as a "how-are-you" greeting by old and young of both sexes, takes on special significance when used by a male to court a female. Bowed forward, bill pointing to the ground, the suitor walks jauntily right past the female. Stopping with his back to her, he raises his bill to the sky and stretches his flippers to the front. He holds the pose for a few seconds, then glances back to see the female's reaction. If she is interested, she may bow in return and the two will begin preening each other.

But the drama has just begun. The female is sure to have other suitors for there are usually more males than females. She can afford to be choosy and may take several days to make her selection. The courting activities are further complicated by immature birds who mimic the love antics of the adults; following them around and sometimes bowing to the female of a mated pair. They may get smacked by a flipper for their daring.

Once a partnership has been formed, the two birds set about the critical and often difficult task of finding a suitable nest site. Some previously mated couples, like the hollow-tree pair, maintain and defend the same nest year after year or establish a new one nearby. Others change sites every year.

Shelter, seclusion and a solid back are the three features a hoiho nest must have for the penguins to breed successfully. The ideal nest is secreted away in the cool, leafy greenness of coastal forest. Here the family will be shielded from the heat of the sun and from wind-driven storms. The moist, dense underbrush offers some protection against predators, such as cats and ferrets, which dislike dampness and prefer to hunt on dry, open land. Because the hoiho's need for isolation is so strong, a couple may fail to raise a family unless their nest is separate from and completely out of sight of other nests. One of the ways the penguins achieve this seclusion is by placing the nest up against something solid, like a log, rock, bank or trunk of a tree. This provides a visual screen as well as a kind of "back-door" security for the penguin in the nest.

While nesting havens that meet these requirements are now hard to find, especially on the mainland, yellow-eyed penguins remain loyal to their long-established breeding grounds, which are near good fishing areas. Tenaciously they search for nest sites in whatever vegetation remains, sometimes traveling long distances from the sea. And they end up in an astonishing variety of places.

Penguins landing on one beach trudge up steep dunes, an exhausting hot trek punctuated by backsliding and belly flops in the sand, to reach their nests in the scrub at the top. After coming ashore in a craggy cove one pair makes a grueling ascent up a headland to a scrap of a nest sandwiched under a rocky overhang. Another nest is wedged out of sight in a huddle of huge boulders, while the massive roots of a fallen tree

provide a sheltered site on exposed pastureland. A thicket of flax plants near the shore suits one couple, but another pair has moved into a deserted stone hut high on a hillside half a mile inland. The vegetation is so sparse in one breeding area that some penguins are living in wooden boxes supplied by a lighthouse keeper.

Each pair of birds calmly goes about preparing their solitary nest, cushioning it with leaves, twigs and grass. This task, like all hoiho family duties, is shared by both mates with neither sex dominating. Other penguins seeking nests seldom interfere, but the two will defend their site if

The hoiho once flourished along forested coastlands, but today their numbers are dwindling. Stoically they nest wherever they can find shelter and seclusion on the predator-infested cleared land.

necessary. Because these peaceful yellow-eyed birds avoid confrontation whenever possible, they rely primarily on threats, such as a menacing glare or a few squawks, to discourage trespassers. A flipper-flapping chase may be used as a last resort, but physical contact is rarely made. How unlike the crowded, rowdy Adelie colonies where couples must fight fiercely to defend their small stony nests from aggressive, pebble-snatching neighbors.

Cloistered away in the privacy of their nest, the hollow-tree couple are very attentive to each other. They often interrupt the gathering of nesting

material to sing duets and nuzzle each other gently with their bills. During this stage the female spends more time fishing than her partner does. She must provide nourishment for herself and for the eggs she will soon lay. The male, who is ready to mate before the female is, tends to stay around the nest waiting patiently. Some days he doesn't go to sea at all. When the female indicates her readiness to mate, the male mounts her, rests his neck on the back of her neck and presses his gently vibrating flippers along her sides. Then he fertilizes the two eggs that have been developing inside her. It is the female who spends the most time at the nest as the time for egg-laying draws near, about twelve days later.

Penguins who live in the close company of colonies respond to group stimulation and the stages of their breeding cycle are highly *synchronized*, so that each pair of birds does things at about the same time as all the others. But the noncolonial yellow-eyed penguins have a more individual time schedule. Egg-laying, for example, ranges from early September to mid-October and incubation may take from thirty-nine to fifty-one days.

The hollow-tree female lays the first of her two greenish-white eggs on September 21, the spring equinox. When the second egg is laid four days later, the long incubation period begins, ensuring the eggs will hatch within hours of each other. The mates take turns incubating the two eggs, which at three-by-two inches are about the size of goose eggs. Although the incubating bird makes frequent yawning stretches, it will not leave the nest unless forced to by heat stress or intruders. If frightened, a penguin may unwittingly smash an egg or roll it out of the nest.

Finally the many hours of constant, careful incubation are rewarded. After forty-three days the eggs are ready to hatch. It takes about forty-eight hours for each chick to peck out of its shell using the egg tooth at the end of its bill. On November 3, just a few hours apart, the damp bundles of dark wispy down, with eyes tightly closed, wriggle free. The tiny three-ounce chicks are weak from their ordeal and completely help-less. They can neither stand nor hold their heads up. But in a few days the gray eyes are wide open and the chicks begin to fidget about, making soft peeping noises. For the first two weeks they are completely hidden from view beneath the parent's breast where they are kept warm and safe.

Young oyster catchers are just hours old when they leave the nest to

By performing the greeting ceremony, preening each other, molting together, defending their nest and caring for their young, the penguin parents maintain their love bond year-round.

Below: The chicks snuggle for a snooze under their watchful parent's flipper.

scurry down the shore after their foraging parents, who feed the chicks as they go along. At two to three weeks old, gull chicks are already learning to swim in the rolling sea swells as they wait for their parents to return with food; and the young Adelie penguins dive into the freezing antarctic water to fend for themselves when they are just six to seven weeks old. The hoiho chicks, however, are confined to the nest area for a very long time, about four months, before they are ready to enter the sea.

For the first six weeks, called the *guard stage*, the parents take turns caring for and feeding their helpless young. One parent stays at the nest all day guarding the chicks while the other fishes, returning in the evening with food. Since a penguin's diet comes entirely from the sea, the hollow-tree chicks do not eat the insects, berries or plants that are so plentiful around the nest. They are fed freshly caught fish and squid which are carried to the nest in the parent's *crop*, a stomach-like sack, and then regurgitated as a partially digested soup. For the first few days the chicks must be coaxed with gentle nudges to take the meal.

The chicks' wobbly heads disappear into the parent's large bill as they feed on the regurgitated seafood soup.

The chicks grow rapidly with daily feedings. Curious and restless, they begin peeking out from under the brooding parent. Soon they are crawling about the nest making tottering attempts to stand up. Little squeaks spurt from the stubby gray bills when they are hungry. Before long they have mastered the upright stance. Bulbous bellies resting on the ground, the plump, fluffy chicks look like they would bounce right back up if they fell over. Flapping their flippers for balance, they take stumbling steps on their large webbed feet and have playful pecking bouts with each other. The spring days are warm and the chicks quickly tire of toddling about. They sprawl out near their attentive parent, who preens the dense light-brown down that has replaced the sparse, darker primary down. The chicks will soon learn to do this job for themselves.

25

Hoiho parents do not have effective defenses to protect their young from predators. On some mainland breeding grounds the chick mortality rate is 60 to 100 percent annually.

Even though their parents guard them continuously during these first six weeks, the hoiho chicks are in great danger. Feral cats, stoats and ferrets hunt on the breeding grounds and follow the well-trodden trails splattered with white excreta to the isolated nests. Hearing a strange noise nearby, the guard parent will make a short inquiry call. If there is no answer, it will take up a protective stance over the chicks. When threatened, the parent will not abandon its young but will regard the intruder with a curious, yellow-eyed stare. It has little experience in defending itself or its chicks, and is totally unprepared for the lightning attacks of these savage predators. A few squawks of anger and a peck of the bill or a swat of a flipper will not prevent a chick from being snatched right from under its bewildered parent.

As the hollow-tree chicks get older and bigger, their individual personalities begin to show. One is more adventurous while the other is more playful and stays closer to the nest. Both are becoming more assertive. And by late afternoon they are very hungry and a bit short-tempered.

One rainy evening as the rising chorus of greeting calls dispels the daytime quiet of the breeding ground, the threesome at the hollow tree are listening for the mother penguin's familiar cry. The chicks' small ears, which are hidden beneath the head feathers, provide them with a keen sense of hearing, and they have already learned to recognize their parents' voices. They wait, but the mother penguin fails to come home at the usual time. The hungry chicks hover around their father, begging with little pecks at his belly, feet and tail. Patiently he ignores their squabbling and preens his coat.

The devoted hoiho parents share equally in rearing their young. The guard parent patiently deals with the hungry, pestering chicks until its mate gets home to feed them.

As the full fury of the storm hits and sheets of rain sweep the breeding ground, the chicks huddle in the dry hollow of the tree. But the father grows more and more anxious; both at sea and on land there are many dangers for a lone penguin. Finally he ventures down the trail and gives a loud yell. Then he shuffles back to check on the chicks. Back and forth, back and forth he goes, waiting for his mate. Then suddenly she rushes in through the drenched tangle of ferns and shrubs that barricades the nest. With a vibrant cry, the father welcomes her. Immediately the two of them launch into an exhilarating "hello" which lasts a full ten minutes. As soon as the greeting is over, the *change of guard* takes place, and the father is relieved of nest duty. Then the mother feeds the squealing chicks who have clambered out of the hollow. Night swallows the dwindling rain, and the family settles down as the "more–pork, more–pork" call of *ruru*, the morepork owl, echoes through the glistening forest.

Soon it is the summer solstice, December 21, the longest day of the year, and the chicks are just over six weeks old. They now have such voracious appetites that both parents must forage at sea every day until the chicks fledge at about fifteen weeks old. During this *post guard stage*, the chicks are left alone at the nest for most of the day. Their colonial cousins, the Adelie chicks, have quite a different post guard experience. At just three weeks of age they gather in a *crèche*, a group of 100 or more chicks plus a few adults, for communal protection against enemies and storms.

The hollow-tree parents leave the nest early and trek down to the shore through the cool dawn as the trilling calls of penguins crisscross the headlands. On the landing rock they join other penguins in a yawning-stretching-preening ritual while they wait for the morning light to spread across the sea. Only when the water is light enough will their white and dark coats provide the camouflage they need to fish and elude enemies.

A penguin's coat is perfectly designed to protect this seafaring bird in another crucial way. It is very warm and completely waterproof, a kind of raincoat, windbreaker and down parka all in one. Thousands of short, curved, oily feathers which overlap at the tips, form a thick watertight garment that covers the entire body. The down at the base of the feathers makes up a dense inner "vest" that keeps the skin dry and prevents the warm air near the body from escaping. In addition to this double-layered "suit," a thick padding of fat just under the skin further insulates the penguin against heat loss. Thus equipped, penguins are better prepared than any other bird to survive in extremely cold water and freezing temperatures.

However, these well-dressed birds sometimes get too warm, especially those that live in tropical or temperate climates. Like other warm-blooded animals they must be able to get rid of heat as well as conserve it, in order to maintain a constant body temperature. Penguins do not sweat, but panting, much the way a dog does, helps them to cool off. Fluffing out the feathers to expose the warm skin to the air is another effective cooling-down technique. Penguins also have the ability to *radiate,* or expel, heat from places on the body where there are few or no feathers. These areas, such as the underside of the flippers and the upper surface of the webbed feet, are flushed with warm blood and then exposed to the air, which facilitates heat loss. This is why yellow-eyed penguins often stand for long periods of time holding their flippers out as though about to take off, and why their flesh-colored feet become such a brilliant pink as they move about on land.

A penguin's survival in the icy sea depends on its waterproof coat being in excellent condition. The hoiho, like all other penguins, must spend a

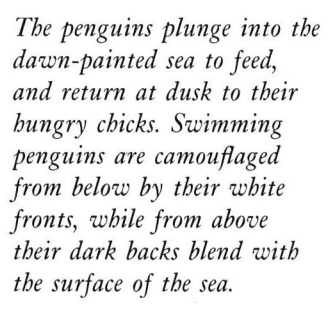

The penguins plunge into the dawn-painted sea to feed, and return at dusk to their hungry chicks. Swimming penguins are camouflaged from below by their white fronts, while from above their dark backs blend with the surface of the sea.

lot of time *preening,* to keep the feathers cleaned, well-oiled and tightly locked together. Penguins appear rather stiff, but their necks are surprisingly free moving, and they look like dancers limbering up as they preen from the tips of their tails to the ends of their flippers. The bill is used to pick up oil from a gland just above the base of the tail, and then like a comb to waterproof and order the plumage. A rubbing movement with the back of the head also helps to spread the oil and smooth the feathers. The penguins assist each other in this essential grooming task by preening each other, especially around the hard-to-reach head and neck areas. Because the feathers wear out and lose their waterproofness, this remarkable coat is completely replaced once a year during the three-week-long molt.

Finally the ocean is light enough and the penguins dive, jump, flop and hop into the churning rush of the surf. Instantly they are transformed from portly upright creatures of the land into streamlined swimming marvels of the sea. The penguin's sleek, solid, elongated body, swiftly propelled by powerful flippers, skims through the water with little friction. Unlike most aquatic birds, such as ducks and cormorants, penguins do not use their webbed feet for paddling but only for braking and steering. The wide feet pressed flat against the short pointed tail make an ideal rudder, allowing the swimmer to turn sharply as it dodges and darts while pursuing its prey or escaping enemies. Although submerged completely while "flying" through the water, penguins often make porpoise-like leaps which may carry them three feet or more through the air. This technique of knifing in and out of the water allows the penguin to breathe without reducing its speed. While porpoising is an effective way to outmaneuver a pursuer, penguins also seem to enjoy leaping from wave to wave just for the fun of it.

Yellow-eyed penguins may reach speeds of ten to fifteen miles per hour as they travel to and from their feeding grounds some four to nine miles from shore. Sometimes this penguin dives to depths of 300 feet to catch a variety of small fish and squid.

The hoiho's powerful hooked bill that is used with such meticulous care to groom the feathers or gently caress a mate, now becomes a razor-sharp tool for grasping fish. The mouth and tongue are lined with fleshy backward-pointing spines that hold the slippery catch which the penguin

swallows whole. Penguins take in large quantities of salt as they fish, and can even drink salt water. A special nasal gland above the eye collects the surplus salt from the body. It is then discharged through the nostrils.

Yellow-eyed penguins tend to fish alone or in twos or threes rather than in large groups. Because of their agility and speed, they can usually outswim predators or escape with only an injury. Some penguins carry the scars from such encounters for the rest of their lives. But there is another danger in the sea from which there is no escape. If a penguin is caught in a fishing net, such as the "walls of death" drift nets or set nets, it will be unable to surface for air and will drown. The death of one parent at the post guard stage in the breeding cycle means certain death by starvation for one of the chicks. A single parent cannot provide enough food for two demanding young penguins.

Yellow-banded heads appear and disappear in the surging green swells as the porpoising penguins head for shore in the late afternoon. Because of their exceptional eyesight, penguins can recognize friends as well as enemies from quite a distance. If a parent, winging its way home, spots a stranger on the landing area, it will delay coming ashore to feed its chicks until the danger has passed.

While their parents are out fishing, the chicks spend the long summer days alternating between restless activity and bouts of sleep. At first the chicks stay snuggled in the cozy hollow. Then, cautiously, they set out to explore the world around the old tree. Soon the fern-strewn forest floor resonates with the flat-footed thumpings of the rotund adventurers. Traipsing up and down hillocks, peering into mossy caverns and tunneling through leafy passageways, the chicks follow each other around. Coming to a halt they stretch, bills open, into silent pantomimes of calls, flap their flippers vigorously or preen themselves and each other—each gesture learned by imitating their parents. The chicks are curious about anything that moves and practice using their now sharp bills by sparring with wind-gyrating vines, snatching at falling leaves or poking at insects crawling about in the forest litter. Frequent yawns reveal the fleshy spines that are developing in the mouth and on the tongue. But in spite of all their comings and goings, the chicks keep amazingly quiet and make only soft peepings now and then. Any strange noise will send them tromping deep

Left on their own all day while their parents feed at sea, the curious chicks explore the nest area.

into the brown and green world of the forest where they are well camouflaged in their light brown coats.

Suddenly, tired from all their walkabouts and play, the chicks flop down with their gray webbed feet stretched out to let the heat escape through the soles. Then, with a start, the next surge of energy hits them and they are off again. High above their heads is the wing-whirring rush of *kukupa*, a large wood pigeon, flying from tree to tree gorging on berries. *Piwakawaka*, a fantail, flits around the nest in a tail-spreading dance catching insects on the wing. And the melodious harmonics of *korimako*, a honey-eating bellbird, chime through the forest. As the post guard stage continues, the chicks may meet up with other restless wanderers along the trails.

Wind-howling storms frequently lash the coast, but the chicks of this breeding ground are fairly well protected. The drenching rain is filtered to splatterings by the dense canopy of leaves and the wind dwindles to a swishing of ferns. On hot days they can easily escape the heat of the sun in the maze of vines and shrubs or under the umbrella of a tree fern. However, chicks at exposed nests on heavily grazed pastureland are extremely vulnerable. With only their feet to act as radiators, the down-covered, panting chicks suffer from heat stress and sometimes die. Defenseless, with no place to hide, they are easily ravaged by dogs that roam the breeding grounds.

By late afternoon, the chicks are anxiously awaiting the highlight of their day, the evening meal. It has been almost twenty-four hours since they were last fed. Early in the post guard stage the first parent to return sometimes has difficulty locating the adventurers, who may be stretched out under a log or seeking shade among the ferns. But a short call is enough to rouse the chicks who come tumbling from their hiding places in a hungry hurry. Later in the post guard stage, when the chicks are familiar with the routine, they sometimes venture down the trail toward the sea to loll about in the summer grass while waiting for their dinner.

The two companions who have gotten along so well during the day now become bickering beggars as they compete for the first mouthful of food. At ten weeks old the plump chicks are almost as tall as their parents and have ravenous appetites. Squealing with bills wide open, they besiege their parent, who in the midst of the fray finally gets a chance to feed first one and then the other. When the second parent arrives on the scene there is no opportunity for the mates to perform the leisurely greeting ceremony of the guard stage. They must be content with a trill or two. Even after the chicks are well-fed with more than a pound of food each, they pursue their parents around the nest pestering for more. Satisfied and sleepy, the chicks finally settle down, and the exhausted parents have time to rest. Soon it will be dawn again.

The demanding daily schedule is beginning to take its toll on the parents. Every afternoon after a long day of fishing, they make the grueling hike up the steep headland carrying extra food for the chicks. There is no time to linger on the landing rock or socialize. Even preening must wait until the chicks are fed. In order for the young penguins to survive their first months at sea, they must have reserves of fat to keep them from starving as they learn to fish for themselves.

After molting into their new waterproof juvenile plumage, the hoiho chicks will plunge individually into the cold dangerous sea for the first time.

However, the chicks' increased demand for food is due not only to their rapid growth but also to a miraculous change taking place. The short, oily feathers that will make up their waterproof coat have been slowly growing out of the down-covered skin. For several days, as the brown-colored down begins to fall out revealing shiny new plumage, the chicks are a raggedy patchwork of fluff and feathers. Finally the new coats are complete and the young penguins are ready for the dramatic change from well-fed chicks on land to self-sustaining juveniles who must fend for themselves at sea.

In late February or early March the hoiho chicks enter the cold South Pacific for the first time. Nearly four months old, they are as tall as their parents and weigh from fourteen to sixteen pounds. In their white and slate-blue juvenile plumage they look similar to adults, but they don't yet have the band of bright yellow feathers around the head or the characteristic yellow eyes. They will not molt into adult plumage until they are about sixteen months old.

One hollow-tree chick leaves for the sea on February 24, and the other on the twenty-eighth. Like many hoiho chicks their entire lives have been lived inland. All they know of the watery world they are entering are the salty meals of fish and the ever present rumble of the surf. They have learned what they can from their parents: the art of careful preening, communication skills and life at the nest. And they have spent weeks trundling about on their large webbed feet. But none of this has prepared them for the sudden initiation into the cold dangerous world of the sea.

They start out plump and healthy, and by instinct they will know what to do with their narrow, flat wings. But only through practice will they become expert at swimming, diving and catching food. While little is known about this stage in the life of the yellow-eyed penguin, it appears that they spend most of the next three to four months at sea, coming ashore infrequently to rocky bays or sandy beaches. Some travel as far as 300 miles north along the coast in search of good winter feeding grounds while others stay nearer home. Those that survive the perils of the open sea—escaping enemies, avoiding fishing nets and finding enough food to stay alive—may return to their home breeding ground in June, July or August to begin a sedentary life.

After the young penguins have departed, the thin, tired, scruffy-looking parents have just three to four weeks to fatten up for the long ordeal to come. With so much swimming and diving in the salty water and regular preening, the feathers of a penguin's coat wear out and must be replaced. Unlike most birds, the sea-feeding penguins cannot renew their plumage gradually. The whole coat must be replaced at one time. The yearly event of growing in new feathers and shedding the old ones is called the *molt*.

For the three weeks that it takes yellow-eyed penguins to complete this transformation they are extremely vulnerable. Without their waterproof protection they are confined to land and must *fast,* living on the fat they have stored up. If frightened into the sea by curious humans or romping dogs, the penguins will soon die from exposure. Weakened by hunger, with their coats in shabby condition, the hoiho must have a shady, secluded place or nest, where they can rest undisturbed. In a forest habitat the molting birds can hide, almost invisible, among the leafy shadows. The many mainland penguins who do not have such havens are easy targets

for sharpshooters or predators and are exposed to harsh coastal weather.

Yellow-eyed penguins do not molt simultaneously at a communal site. From late February when the chicks, juveniles and nonbreeding adults begin their molt, until early May when most breeding adults have finished, there are penguins molting, alone or in pairs, somewhere on the breeding grounds.

By the time of the autumn equinox, March 21, the hollow-tree pair have retreated to their nest. Like most devoted hoiho couples they will only return to the sea together, after both of them have finished the uncomfortable molt. Patiently they pass the time sleeping, stretching, rubbing off the old plumage and crooning softly to each other. By the end of the three weeks the bedraggled, miserable-looking penguins, with tufts of tattered feathers and painfully swollen flippers, have been transformed into handsome, princely figures. They are decked out in shimmering new plumage—a snowy-white breast, shiny slate-blue back, gold and black feathered crown and brilliant yellow headband. But the penguins have lost about eight pounds, nearly half their body weight. Fully waterproofed again, they are more than ready to dive into the sea to feed.

Now begins the most social season for this least social of penguins. With the breeding season and the molt behind them, the hoiho feed at sea everyday to replenish their fat reserves. After scrambling ashore in the late afternoon they join their fellows in a leisurely grooming session. Some, who are seeking mates, engage in the antics of courtship. Occasionally a squabble breaks out between two birds, but it doesn't last for long. The hoiho has devised a successful way to avoid a fight: the opponents turn away from each other and resort to vigorous preening as a face-saving device.

Soon it is the winter solstice, June 21, the shortest day of the year. The seething waves that crash along the shore in stormy weather can be treacherous. Sometimes the penguins make several attempts before they land successfully on the slippery, wave-battered rock. When two companions ride in together and one has difficulty landing, the other one will dive in again and accompany its friend ashore.

On less blustery days the penguins paddle playfully in the stream, splashing each other with their flippers and dunking in and out of the water in a kind of hide-and-seek. This popular pastime is also very beneficial. The freshwater bath helps clean the feathers and provides fresh drinking water. Others who are less boisterous snooze in the thin winter sunlight or loaf about among the tree ferns and bracken. But with their keen eyesight and excellent hearing, the hoiho are constantly alert to danger. A shrill warning cry from a penguin who has sighted an intruder will send those near the sea plunging into the waves.

During the winter months the juveniles return, one by one, to their home breeding grounds. But less than half the chicks that were fledged survive their months at sea. In the years when there is a shortage of fish and squid there will be even fewer.

Although most of the juveniles now begin their sedentary life, fishing during the day and spending nights ashore, they still have much to learn

about being a penguin. As with most seabirds the highest mortality of young yellow-eyed penguins is in the first two years of life. Only fifteen percent will make it to breeding age, two to three years old for females and three to five for males.

Back on their home breeding grounds, the juveniles, who have only themselves to feed and care for, have a lot of time for leisurely preening, loitering and practicing calls and courtship behavior. Sometimes one juvenile will team up with another or with an unmated bird, who may become its partner in the future. In the late afternoon when the adults come ashore, the juveniles often rush up to greet them with bows. Frequently they tag along with a mated pair, possibly their parents, to a nest site where they stand quietly nearby without interfering.

Soon it is September again and the busy but perilous breeding season is well under way as the hoiho couples prepare for egg laying. Settled in

Conservation-minded individuals work to help the hoiho survive. Fencing keeps livestock out of the breeding grounds, and flax plants provide nesting shelter. Some hoiho have lived for twenty years, but currently the average age is nine because of the threats it faces on land and at sea.

their well-hidden nest, the hollow-tree pair joins the exuberant evening chorus of trills and calls ringing through the spring twilight.

But how much longer will the hoiho, the world's rarest penguin, be able to survive? Recently New Zealanders have become aware of the serious plight of this extraordinary penguin with whom they share their homeland. They are determined that the name "hoiho" will never be added to the growing list of extinct species. An amazingly diverse group of people—including farmers, fishermen, homemakers, college students, school children, tour guides, teachers, business people and politicians as well as scientists and environmentalists—is at work to save the hoiho. Their concern reflects a growing worldwide recognition that our planet is one complex *ecosystem,* a natural living system in which all things from the most minute organisms to the largest mammals are inextricably linked to each other and to the environment they share.

To ensure the survival of the yellow-eyed penguin on the mainland as well as on offshore islands, a major recovery and management program has been launched by New Zealand's Department of Conservation in conjunction with the Royal Forest and Bird Protection Society, the Yellow-eyed Penguin Trust and the World Wide Fund for Nature. The success of the program depends on adequate funds and an enormous commitment of time and energy on the part of individuals. The rescue of the hoiho, as with any species, depends on an *ecological* approach which considers the interaction of the penguin with its habitats, both land and sea, and with the plants and animals that share them. Because scientists have been studying the behavior and biology of this unique penguin for years, conservationists believe they know what will most help the hoiho in its struggle to survive.

Although the yellow-eyed penguin is protected by law under the Wildlife Act of 1953, its habitats are not. The first priority, then, has been to establish large reserves to accommodate the hoiho's solitary nesting habits. Once the reserves are created, they must be securely fenced to keep grazing stock out and to discourage humans and their dogs from entering the breeding grounds.

Without constant grazing, the vegetation will slowly begin to regenerate. But a massive replanting effort is needed to provide the penguin with the shelter it urgently requires. Winter, the nonbreeding season, is the best time to restore the reserves. Volunteers, many of whom are students, have already started planting flax, shrubs and native trees. A bonus of revegetation efforts will be the return of other native birds to the coast, many of whom have not been seen or heard since the forests were destroyed.

Attempts are being made to control the *Mustilid* and feral cat populations. While totally eliminating predators by trapping and other means is impossible, their numbers can be reduced. The long-term plan, however, is to discourage rabbits and their predators from entering the penguins' breeding grounds by planting buffer zones of thick vegetation around the penguin reserves.

The ecological approach must also consider the impact of human visitors on the penguins and their habitats. Wildlife tourism has become a flourishing business, and the penguin is one of the animals people most want to see. Although most people would not willingly harm a penguin, out of ignorance they sometimes cause irreparable damage. A vital part of the management program has been to set guidelines for viewing these timid, easily frightened birds. Observation platforms, or bird hides, far removed from the penguins' activity, equipped with information about the hoiho and monitored by the Department of Conservation, will be established at a few select sites. The protection of the penguin, not the entertainment of people, is the main concern.

Marine reserves which are being planned for coastal zones adjacent to the breeding grounds may help safeguard the hoiho's marine habitat. Unfortunately these reserves will not extend far enough out to sea to include *Megadyptes*' major feeding grounds.

Funding further research and educating the public are other essential aspects of the "save the hoiho" campaign. By making information on the hoiho and the perils it faces available to the public, scientists can work toward a better understanding of what needs to be done to help the species survive, and what individuals can do to help.

Even though the recovery program is now under way, time is running out for the hoiho, whose population is declining every year. New Zealanders must act swiftly to ensure that the trilling, sky-piercing calls of the hoiho, penguin of the forest, continue to ring above the roar of the sea as they have for millions of years.

Index